Destination Detectives

Brazil

North America

Europe

Asia

BRAZIL

Africa

South America

Australasia

Ali Brownlie Bojang

Raintree

D0552996

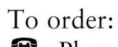

www.raintreepublishers.co.uk

Visit our website to find out more information about **Raintree** books.

To order:

☎ Phone 44 (0) 1865 888112

🖹 Send a fax to 44 (0) 1865 314091

🖥 Visit the Raintree Bookshop at **www.raintreepublishers.co.uk** to browse our catalogue and order online.

First published in Great Britain by Raintree,
Halley Court, Jordan Hill, Oxford OX2 8EJ,
Part of Harcourt Education.
Raintree is a registered trademark of
Harcourt Education Ltd.

© Harcourt Education Ltd 2007
The moral right of the proprietor has been asserted.

Produced for Raintree Publishers by Discovery Books Ltd
Editorial: Kathryn Walker, Sonya Newland,
Melanie Waldron, and Lucy Beevor
Design: Clare Nicholas, and Rob Norridge
Picture Research: Amy Sparks
Production: Chloe Bloom
Originated by Modern Age
Printed and bound in China
By South China Printing Company

10 digit ISBN 1 4062 0720 9 (hardback)
13 digit ISBN 978 1 4062 0720 0
10 9 8 7 6 5 4 3 2 1
11 10 09 08 07

10 digit ISBN 1 4062 0727 6 (paperback)
13 digit ISBN 978 1 4062 0727 9
10 9 8 7 6 5 4 3 2 1
11 10 09 08 07

British Library Cataloguing in Publication Data
Brownlie Bojang, Ali, 1949-
    Brazil. - (Destination Detectives)
    1. Brazil. - Geography - Juvenile literature 2. Brazil -
    Social life and customs - 21st century - Juvenile literature
    3. Brazil - Civilization - Juvenile literature
    I. Title
    981'.065

This levelled text is a version of *Freestyle:
Destination Detectives: Brazil*, produced for Raintree
Publishers by White-Thomson Publishing Ltd.

Acknowledgements
Corbis pp. 6b (Sergio Pitamitz), 9 (Paulo Fridman), 10–11
(Pierre Merimee), 18 (Archivo Iconografico, S.A.), 20–21
(Jeremy Horner), 21 (Jamil Bittar/Reuters), 22 (Reuters),
25b (Stephanie Maze), 26 (Silvio Avila/Reuters), 33 (Fabio
Polenghi), 36 (Ricardo Azoury); Corbis Sygma pp. 8 (Collart
Herve), 12 (Collart Herve), 14; Photolibrary pp. 4–5 (Jon
Arnold Images), 5t (Index Stock Imagery), 5m (Berndt
Fischer), 5b (Workbook, Inc.), 6t (Berndt Fischer), 11
(Olivier Grunewald), 13 (Digital Vision), 15 (Jon Arnold
Images), 16 (Olivier Grunewald), 17 (Jon Arnold Images),
23 (Workbook, Inc.), 24 (Jon Arnold Images), 25t (Index
Stock Imagery), 28, 38 (Edward Parker), 40 (Berndt Fischer),
41t (Olivier Grunewald), 41b (Olivier Grunewald); South
American Pictures pp. 19 (Tony Morrison), 27 (Jason P.
Howe), 29 (Tony Morrison), 30 (Tony Morrison), 31 (Tony
Morrison), 32 (Tony Morrison), 34 (Tony Morrison), 37
(Tony Morrison), 39 (Tony Morrison), 42 (Tony Morrison);
TopFoto pp. 35, 43.

Cover photograph of Rio Carnival reproduced
with permission of Photolibrary/Workbook, Inc.

Thanks to Rhian Evans and Simon Scoones

Contents

KT-525-191

Any words appearing in the text in bold, **like this,** are explained in the glossary. You can also look out for them in the Word Bank box at the bottom of each page.

Where in the world?

Brazilwood tree

Brazil got its name from a redwood tree. The tree is named *pau brazil*. This means "brazilwood".

The first Brazilian people were the **Amerindians**. They painted their faces with dye from this tree.

The plane shudders. You open your eyes with a start. You look out of the window. The plane is flying past green mountains. The mountain peaks are a long way above you!

Now the plane flies near the ocean. You can see beautiful beaches. Wide streets are lined with palm trees. There are lots of luxury homes here.

This is the city of Rio de Janeiro. It has a beautiful harbour.

➤

4   **WORD BANK**   **Amerindian** person whose ancestors were the first people to live in South America

Next you see high-rise buildings. How can the plane land? There are so many buildings here. Suddenly the landing strip appears. It is on a platform that juts out into the sea.

You land with a gentle bump. The plane has arrived at Santos Dumont Airport. You are now in Brazil's most exciting city. This is Rio de Janeiro!

Find out later...

...where you can find this giant statue.

...where in Brazil you can see hundreds of rare animals and birds.

...which city hosts the biggest carnival in the world.

5

This is Brazil

At the airport you buy a map and a guidebook. You see straight away that Brazil is the biggest country in South America. You begin to make some notes.

Brazil at a glance

SIZE: 8.5 million square kilometres (3.3 million square miles)

CAPITAL: Brasília

POPULATION: 186 million

LANGUAGE: Portuguese

CURRENCY: Real, written R$

The Pantanal is a huge area of **wetlands** and swamps. These are places where the ground is very watery. The Pantanal is home to many **species** (types) of animals. They include a type of alligator known as the Cayman (above).

Natal is in northeastern Brazil. Giant sand dunes are a big attraction. So is the tasty seafood.

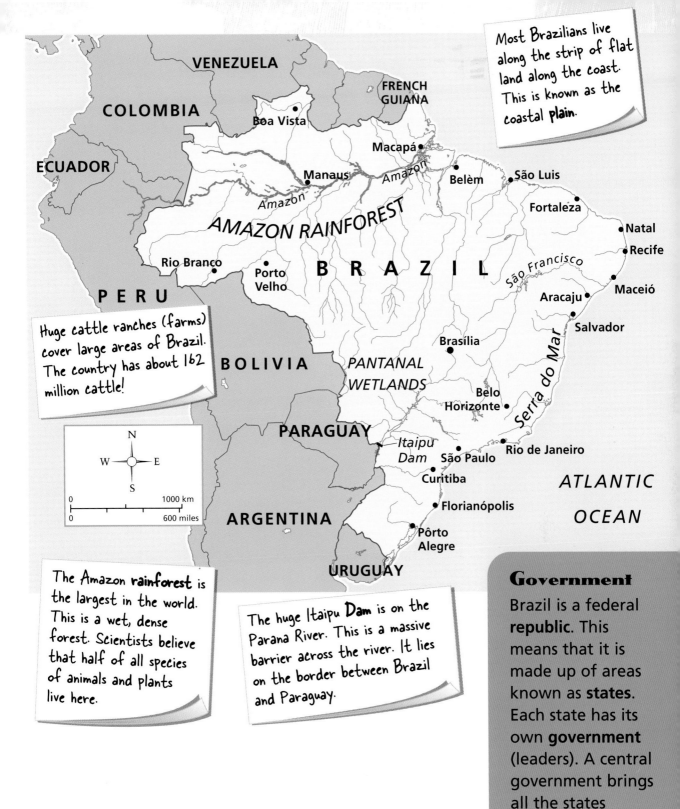

Most Brazilians live along the strip of flat land along the coast. This is known as the coastal **plain**.

Huge cattle ranches (farms) cover large areas of Brazil. The country has about 162 million cattle!

The Amazon **rainforest** is the largest in the world. This is a wet, dense forest. Scientists believe that half of all species of animals and plants live here.

The huge Itaipu **Dam** is on the Parana River. This is a massive barrier across the river. It lies on the border between Brazil and Paraguay.

Government

Brazil is a federal **republic**. This means that it is made up of areas known as **states**. Each state has its own **government** (leaders). A central government brings all the states together. The United States is also a federal republic.

government group of people that makes laws and manages the country

Getting around

Brazil is the fifth-largest country in the world. There are huge distances to travel. Parts of Brazil have very few roads.

Long-distance travel

There are lots of long-distance buses. On some of them you can get a sleeper. This is a seat that stretches out to make a bed.

You can travel by boat along the Amazon River. Passengers can sleep in cabins or on the deck.

This is a "tube" bus shelter. Fares are collected in the bus shelter. When the bus pulls in, people can step quickly on board.

The Trans-Amazonian Highway

The **government** has built new roads. They go to **remote** areas of Brazil. These are places far from towns or cities.

The most important of these roads is the Trans-Amazonian Highway. It runs straight through the **Amazon rainforest** (see map, page 7).

The quickest way to cross the country is by plane. Otherwise your journey could take days. Not all Brazilians can afford to fly, though. Most people here travel by bus or car.

Manaus

3,490 km
(2,167 miles)

2,135 km
(1,326 miles) Recife

Salvador
1,446 km
(898 miles)

1,015 km
(630 miles)

1,148 km
(713 miles)

São
Paulo

Rio de
Janeiro

N

W   E

S

0   1000 km

0   600 miles

Brasilia is the capital of Brazil. But it is more than 1,000 kilometres (600 miles) away from any other large city.

This highway stretches 1,600 kilometres (1,000 miles). It links the River Amazon with southern Brazil.

remote   far from other places

Climate and landscape

Brazil is a very large country. Different parts of the country have different **climates** (weather patterns).

Climate

Rainforests cover more than half the country. The weather in these areas is **tropical**. It is always hot. There is always lots of rain. There are about 2,200 millimetres (90 inches) of rainfall each year. This makes the air feel **humid**. It is damp and steamy.

Different seasons

Brazil is at the opposite end of the Earth from the United States and Europe. When it is summer in the United States, it is winter in Brazil.

In the north-east, the landscape is very dry. Only a few shrubs grow here.

Northeastern Brazil can get as hot as 104° F (40° C). But there is little rain. This part of Brazil often has long periods without rain. These periods are known as **droughts**. At these times it is hard for anything to grow.

A mist rises from the damp rainforest.

Temperature extremes

	Minimum	Maximum
Manaus	18°C (64°F)	36°C (97°F)
Belem	21°C (70°F)	34°C (93°F)
São Paulo	5°C (41°F)	34°C (93°F)
Porto Alegre	0°C (32°F)	37°C (99°F)
Brasilia	7°C (45°F)	32°C (90°F)

humid when there is a lot of water vapour in the air

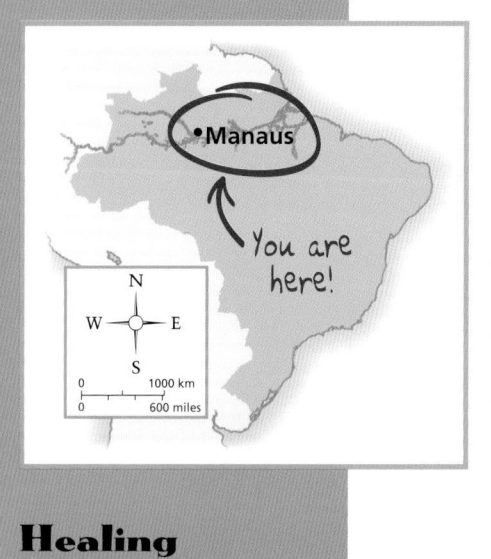

You are here!

The Amazon rainforest

You fly to Manaus (see map on left). This city is in the centre of the Amazon region. At Manaus you go on a boat trip. The boat takes you along the amazing Amazon River.

The Amazon is the second-longest river in the world. It is more than 6,275 kilometres (3,900 miles) long. It runs through the huge **rainforest**.

Healing plants

There are about 55,000 plant species in the Brazilian rainforest. Many of these are used in medicines.

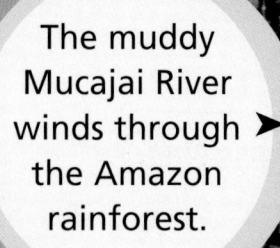

The muddy Mucajai River winds through ➤ the Amazon rainforest.

WORD BANK   canopy covering provided by the tops of trees in forests

You stop for a while. Your guide takes you into the forest. There isn't much light here. The tops of the trees form a thick covering. This is known as the **canopy**.

The rainforest is hot and damp. This makes a perfect home for thousands of **species** (types) of plants and animals. Some live only in the rainforest.

In the last 40 years the rainforest has been badly damaged. People have cut down the trees. This has made room for roads and farming.

Rainforest survival tips

• Piranhas are small fish. But they have very sharp teeth. They will attack anything bleeding in the water.

• Diseases are spread by mosquitos. Some of these diseases can kill. Cover up well!

Millions of rainforest trees have been cleared. Sometimes this is so sand or **minerals** can be dug out of the ground. Minerals include precious stones and metals.

mineral natural substance found in rocks and in the ground. Metals and precious stones are minerals.

13

The Yanomami people like to paint their faces and bodies.

The Yanomami

The Yanomami are a group of Amerindian people. They live in the Amazon rainforest. Yanomami believe that river and forest spirits guide their lives. Their way of life is in danger. Farms and mines are taking over their lands.

Life in the rainforest

In the rainforest you find a small group of **Amerindians**. Amerindians were the first people to live in South America.

You chat with a young woman. She tells you that all her family used to live in small groups like this. These people got all they needed by farming, hunting, and fishing.

In the 1970s the **government** built new roads here. They also made new villages and towns. Since then large areas of rainforest have been cleared. This has made life very hard for her family.

Mining

The Greater Carajas **mine** is in the Amazon rainforest. A mine is where substances such as metals are dug out of the ground. The Greater Carajas mine is huge.

Manaus is the starting point for boat trips along the Amazon River.

Manaus

Manaus is one of the world's largest river **ports**. A port is where ships load and unload. Farming products and goods made in Manaus leave the city every day. They are sold to other countries.

mine hole in the ground from which minerals such as metals, precious stones, or coal are dug

Baby turtles head towards the sea on a Brazilian beach.

The Planalto Brasileiro

There are many other types of landscape in Brazil. A lot of the scenery is very beautiful. South of the Amazon region is the Planalto Brasileiro (see map on left). This is a huge **plateau**. It is a high, flat area. There are cattle ranches and farms here.

A mountain range runs along the eastern edge of the plateau. This is named the Serra do Mar. These mountains run along the coast.

Turtles on the coast

Brazil has nearly 7,500 kilometres (4,660 miles) of coastline. Five **species** (types) of turtle are found here. There are special laws to protect them.

Wetlands

The Pantanal (see map, page 16) is a huge area of **wetlands**. Wetlands are areas of watery land. They have swamps and marshes. Marshes are low-lying wet land.

In the Pantanal you can find the beautiful hyacinth macaw. It is the world's largest parrot. There are also giant river otters and jaguars.

The Caatinga

The northeast has a dry, stony area. It is called the Caatinga. Farmers have to work very hard to make anything grow here.

Iguaçu Falls

The Iguaçu Falls (see map, page 16) are where Brazil meets the country, Argentina. There are about 275 separate falls. Together they are about 3 kilometres (1.8 miles) wide.

The Iguaçu is made up of different waterfalls. They are separated by rocky islands.

species   different types of animals and plants

History and culture

The people you met in the rainforest were **Amerindians**. These people were related to Brazil's first people. Amerindians settled in the country thousands of years ago.

Portuguese influence

In 1500 people from Portugal arrived in Brazil. Portugal is a country in western Europe. The Portuguese took control of the country. They began farming the land.

Amerindians

About 330,000 Amerindians live in the rainforest. There are more than 200 different groups. They have their own customs and languages. Today less than 1 percent of Brazil's population are Amerindians.

This picture was painted in the 18th century. It shows slaves mining diamonds.

But the Portuguese needed people to help them. Between the 16th and 17th centuries they brought millions of slaves to Brazil. A **slave** is someone who is forced to work without pay. These slaves came from West Africa.

More newcomers

More Europeans moved to Brazil in the 19th century. Some worked in the coffee business. Others worked in gold mining.

In the 20th century many Asians settled in Brazil. They worked on farms around São Paulo (see map, page 7). A large number were from Japan.

São Paulo (see map, page 7) has the biggest Japanese population outside of Japan.

Music and dance

Brazil is famous for its music and dance. Brazilian music is a mix of African and European styles. The music can be cool and relaxed. Other types of Brazilian music can be loud and lively.

You hear music everywhere you go in Brazil. The people here are often dancing. Sometimes you see children dancing in the street. You see old men tapping their feet to the music.

Amerindian music

Amerindians have their own type of music. They copy the sounds of the **rainforest**. The Amerindians use rattles and drums to do this. They also use flutes made from reeds.

This band of drummers is from Bahia **state**. Bahia ➤ is in the northeast of Brazil.

Someone tells you that there's a great show of music and dance at Rio de Janeiro. This is the city's world-famous carnival. It takes place each year in February or March. It's about to start now. So you head off to Rio de Janeiro.

Students in Brasilia (see map, page 7) demonstrate capoeira.

Capoeira

Capoeira (above) is a mix of dance and self-defence moves. It was started by African **slaves** in Brazil. Players move in cartwheels and handstands. They attack using only legs, feet, and heads. This is all done to music.

slave   someone who is owned by another person

The carnival

In Rio de Janeiro, you go to the Sambodromo. This is an enormous stadium. It is 700 metres (half a mile) long. The Sambodromo is on either side of a wide avenue. The carnival parade passes along the avenue.

When it gets dark, the carnival begins. **Samba** schools, or clubs, compete with each other. Samba is a traditional Brazilian dance.

This is a samba school float. It is passing through the carnival stadium.

The schools spend months practising for the carnival. They make dazzling costumes. They also build parade **floats**. These are moving stages.

The people leading the schools blow whistles. The bands play. The drums pound. The noise is deafening. Everyone laughs and cheers.

Later on, you wander through the city. You see lots of smaller street parades. This feels like the biggest party in the world!

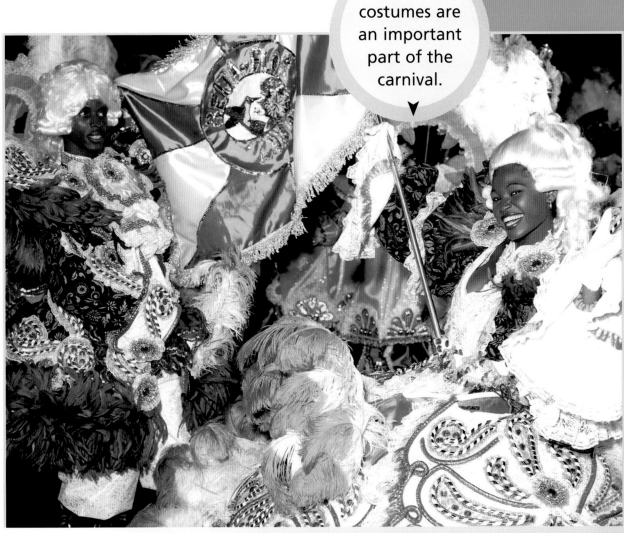

Fabulous costumes are an important part of the carnival.

float platform, or stage, pulled by or built on to a vehicle. It is part of a carnival parade.

Religion

You've noticed lots of old churches in the city centre. Some are about 500 years old. They were built by the Portuguese settlers.

The Portuguese brought **Catholicism** to Brazil. Catholicism is a **Christian** religion. It is based on the teachings of Jesus Christ. Today, more than 70 percent of Brazilians are Catholics. Many people mix other beliefs with Catholicism.

This is the Metropolitan Cathedral in Brasília (see map, page 7). Brasília is famous for its striking modern buildings.

Candomble

Some Brazilians follow a religion called Candomble. This is a mixture of African beliefs and Catholicism. It includes some **Amerindian** customs.

Followers make offerings (gifts) to spirits. These are called *orixas*. But at the same time they make offerings to Jesus. Most followers are African Brazilians. These are Brazilians who have some African blood.

Christ the Redeemer

A giant statue of Jesus (above) looks down on Rio de Janeiro. This statue is named Christ the Redeemer. It is on Corcovado Mountain. The statue is 30 metres (98 feet) high.

These girls celebrate the festival of the goddess Iemanja. They throw flowers and perfume into the sea for her.

Amerindian person whose ancestors were the first people to live in South America

Everyday life

Rio de Janeiro is famous for its beautiful white beaches. You decide to spend the day on the beach. It seems like everyone is here!

Some people are surfing. Others are playing **volleyball**. Volleyball is very popular in Brazil. Basketball and tennis are also popular sports.

Pelé

Pelé is one of Brazil's most famous footballers. He played for Brazil from the 1950s to the 1970s. Pelé scored more than 1,200 goals during his career.

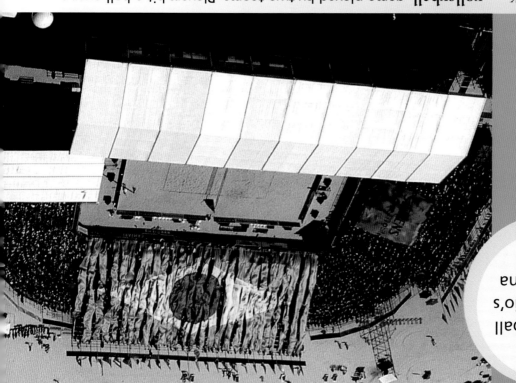

This is the volleyball court on Rio's Copacabana Beach.

Football mad

In the evening you go to a football match.
It is at the Maracana stadium in Rio de Janeiro.
This is the biggest football stadium in the world.

You can see that Brazilians are crazy about
football! Everyone is waving flags. A loud drum
beats all through the match. Every time Brazil
scores, the band plays. Fire
crackers also go off.

Brazilian
football fans
cheer on their
team in the
Maracana
stadium.

Food

Feijoada is Brazil's national dish. It is made with pork and black beans. The first people to make this dish were African **slaves**. They made it with food left over from their owners' meals.

Bahia state is in northeastern Brazil. Bahian food has a strong African flavour. It is quite spicy. Palm oil, hot peppers, and coconut milk are often used in the dishes here.

Daily doughnuts

Bolinho de chuva are traditional doughnuts. You can have them salty or sweet. People eat them at breakfast or tea time.

Feijoada is Brazil's national dish.

WORD BANK slave someone who is owned by another person

Barbecued meat is popular in Brazil. This is known as *churrasco*. The meat is usually soaked in spices and flavourings. Then it is grilled. It is served with rice and *farofa*. *Farofa* is toasted cassava flour. Cassava is a plant root.

Eating habits

In Brazil it is very rude to eat food when you walk down the street. Food should be eaten where you bought it or taken home.

This woman is selling traditional snacks on the street-side.

Going to school

You get up very early the next morning. The friends you are staying with start school at 7.00 a.m. You have breakfast with them. Breakfast is bread rolls with butter, jam, and white cheese. There is also fruit.

In Brazil, children have to go to school between the ages of 7 and 14. Students attend primary school until the age of 14.

These children are leaving a secondary school in Cuiaba. This city is in western Brazil.

WORD BANK   government group of people that makes laws and manages the country

They go to secondary school from the age of 15 to 17. Students have exams at the end of each year.

They have to work hard to pass exams. Children who fail exams have to do the year all over again.

Many children leave school at a young age. They have to work to help their families. Local **governments** and groups try to keep them at school. Sometimes they give the families money if the children go to school.

This primary school is in a poor area of northeastern Brazil.

State and private schools

State schools in Brazil do not get a lot of money. Schools in the country are even poorer than city schools. Many parents try to send their children to private schools. But this costs a lot of money.

Cities of Brazil

It's a beautiful, clear day in Rio de Janeiro. So you take a train to the top of Corcovado Mountain. This stands high above the city.

The view is fantastic. You look down on a city of 11 million people. Rio lies between the sea and the mountains. Most of the buildings here are tall. They are crammed together.

Favelas

You notice the **favelas**, or slums, along some hillsides. These are areas of dirty, overcrowded housing. Some houses are made with cardboard and metal. This is where the poor live.

Growing cities

Brazil has some of the largest cities in the world. Twelve of its cities have populations of more than one million.

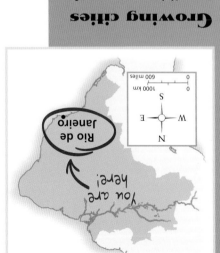

You are here!

Rio de Janeiro

N
W   E
S

0   1000 km
0   600 miles

This is a Brazilian favela. It is the type of housing that poor people live in.

Most Brazilian cities have favelas. The **government** is trying to improve them. Some now have street lights and drains. Many areas have community centres. These are places where local people can gather together.

City locations
Most of Brazil's towns and cities are in the south-east and south. But there are some large cities in the northeast. They include Salvador and Recife (see map, page 7).

Brazilians love football. Children play it in the streets and the favelas.

The streets of Brazil

You notice that a large number of children work on the city streets. In Brazil, poor people do not get any money from the **government**. Poor familes often send their children out to beg. Some children earn money by washing cars. Others clean shoes.

You also notice that Brazilian cities are very busy and noisy. Traffic jams the streets. Car fumes **pollute** the air.

These are some of Brazil's street children. They make money by polishing shoes. ➤

WORD BANK   pollute   to release harmful chemicals or waste into air, water, or soil

Brasilia

Brasilia is Brazil's capital city. It is in the centre of the country (see map, page 9). Brasilia was built in the 1950s. It is famous for its striking modern buildings.

São Paulo

São Paulo (see map, page 7) is the largest city in Brazil. About 20 million people live there. It is a major centre of business and industry (producing goods).

Salvador

The city of Salvador is in the northeast of Brazil (see map, page 7). For hundreds of years, slaves were brought to Salvador from Africa. Today about 80 percent of the city's population are African Brazilians.

Skyscrapers line the streets of São Paulo. This is one of the largest cities in the world.

Living in the countryside

You have seen some of Brazil's busy cities. But what is life like in the **rural** (countryside) areas?

Coffee crops

Farming is the main type of work for people living in the countryside. Many crops are grown to sell in other countries. These are known as cash crops. Coffee is one of Brazil's most important cash crops.

Today Brazil produces 40 percent of the world's coffee. It grows mainly in areas around two cities. These cities are São Paulo and Rio de Janeiro (see map, page 7).

Grown in São Paulo

The **state** of São Paulo is a major farming area. Most of Brazil's oranges are grown here. São Paulo state also produces half of the country's sugar.

This man is picking coffee beans. Brazil produces more coffee beans than any other country.

Ranches on the pampas

In the south and central areas of Brazil there are huge grasslands. These are known as *pampas*.

The *pampas* are ideal places for raising cattle. There are many large ranches (cattle farms) here. Beef has become one of Brazil's most important **exports**. An export is a product sold to other countries.

Gauchos

Brazil has many large cattle ranches. Men on horseback round up the cattle (see picture below). These men are known as *gauchos*. They are similar to American cowboys.

Poorest regions

The poorest parts of Brazil are in the northeast. The land is very dry. The farmers mostly grow vegetables and fruit for themselves. Sometimes they grow cotton to sell. Some years there is very little rainfall. Then it is hard to grow anything.

Minerals

Many important **minerals** are mined in Brazil's countryside. Minerals are natural substances. Metals, such as iron, are minerals.

Iron ore and bauxite are mined here. Iron ore is rock that contains iron. Bauxite contains the metal called aluminium.

A farmer harvests sugar cane. This is in the poor northeastern region of Brazil.

➤

WORD BANK   mineral natural substance found in rocks and in the ground. Metals and precious stones are minerals.

Fishing

Fish is a popular food in Brazil. Most of it is caught by local fishermen. There are a few fishing businesses that use modern equipment.

Fishermen bring their catch of shrimps ashore at Peba. This is a small town by the Atlantic Ocean.

US immigrants

In the last few years, more than 200 US farmers have moved to Brazil. These farmers have sold their farms in the United States. They have joined with others to buy farms in Brazil. Land is cheaper here than in the United States.

Environment and wildlife

The tamarin

The golden-headed lion tamarin is a small monkey. Its home is in the rainforest of northeastern Brazil. Today less than 10 percent of the forest remains. There may be just 200 tamarin monkeys left there.

You are coming to the end of your stay in Brazil. You go to a café with your friends. They tell you how they feel about their country.

They believe they live in one of the most beautiful countries in the world. But they worry about what is happening to the land and animals.

Protecting the rainforest

The **rainforest** is in danger. Many trees have been cut down. This is mainly done to make way for cattle ranches. But without trees, the soil soon dries up.

Tamarin monkeys are very shy. They live high in the tree tops. ➤

WORD BANK   rainforest dense forest that has heavy rainfall

The Brazilian **Environment** Agency has the job of protecting the rainforest. This organization tries to stop people causing damage that is against the law. Special equipment and planes help them watch over this huge area.

The rainforest is home to many types of tree frog.

The hyacinth macaw
The hyacinth macaw (below) is the world's largest parrot. It lives in the Pantanal **wetlands** (see map, page 7). Some people will pay thousands of pounds to have one as a pet.

The hyacinth macaw can grow up to 100 centimetres (40 inches) in length.

environment the natural world or the conditions that surround us

Stay or go?

Your stay in Brazil has come to an end. You've seen the cities and the countryside. You have enjoyed the friendliness of the people here. You could stay longer. There are still many things to see and do here. Will you stay or go?

Other things to do

- See the unusual rock formations and waterfalls of Chapada Diamantina. This is an area in northeastern Brazil.

Tourist hotspot

Brazil is a major tourist destination. Nearly half of all visitors to Brazil pass through Rio de Janeiro.

This is the Opera House in Manaus. It is more than 100 years old.

- Go rock climbing at Bau Rock. It is in the Mantiqueira Mountains of southeastern Brazil.

- Listen to music at the magnificent Opera House in Manaus (see map, page 7).

- Take a boat to the island of Paqueta in Rio de Janeiro bay. There are no cars here.

- Visit the beautiful city of Recife. This is a city of water and bridges. Many of Brazil's most famous artists live in Recife (see map, page 7).

The city of Recife lies in northeastern Brazil. It is on the Atlantic Ocean.

Find out more

Are there ways for a Destination Detective to find out more about Brazil? Yes! Check out the books listed below:

Further reading

The Changing Face of Brazil, Edward Parker (Hodder Wayland, 2001)

Country Files: Brazil, Marion Morrison (Franklin Watts, 2003)

Nations of the World: Brazil, Anita Dalal (Raintree, 2003)

Plants and Planteaters (Secrets of the Rainforest), Michael Chinery (Cherrytree Books, 2000)

Poisoners and Pretenders (Secrets of the Rainforest), Michael Chinery (Cherrytree Books, 2000)

Rainforest (Eye Wonders), Helen Sharman (Dorling Kindersley, 2004)

Rainforest People, Edward Parker (Hodder Wayland, 2002)

World in Focus: Brazil, Simon Scoones (Hodder, 2006)

World Wide Web

If you want to find out more about Brazil you can search the Internet. Try using keywords such as these:

- Brazil
- Rio de Janeiro
- Brasilia
- Amazon rainforest

You can also find your own keywords by using words from this book.
Try using a search directory such as www.yahooligans.com

Timeline

About 3000 BC
First people arrive in Brazil, probably from Asia.

1494
Pope Alexander VI gives Brazil to Portugal.

1500
Portuguese arrive and claim the land.

1530
Brazil becomes a Portuguese colony.

1763
Rio de Janeiro becomes the capital of Brazil.

1822
Independence is declared.

1840
Dom Pedro II becomes emperor of Brazil.

1888
Slavery ends. Many Europeans start to arrive.

1890
Pedro II gives up the throne. Brazil is declared a **republic**. This is a form of **government** where people elect leaders. These leaders govern the country.

1890s
A coffee boom brings in almost 1 million settlers from Europe.

1943–1945
Brazil fights against Germany in World War II.

1960
The capital city is moved to Brasilia.

1964–1985
For 21 years Brazil is ruled by military governments. People are not able to vote.

1977
Brazilian **Amerindians** hold their first national conference.

2000
Brazil celebrates its 500th anniversary as a country.

2002
Brazil wins its fifth football World Cup.

2003
Lula is elected as President of Brazil.

2004
Brazil launches its first space rocket.

Brazil – facts and figures

The Brazilian flag shows the night sky in a yellow diamond. This sits on a green background. The green represents all the forests in the country. The yellow diamond represents the **minerals** that are mined in Brazil. The banner across the circle carries Latin words meaning "order and progress".

People and places

- Population: 186 million.
- Life expectancy:

men – 68

women – 76.

- Brazil is 4,319 km (2,684 miles) wide at its widest. It stretches 4,395 kilometres (2,730 miles) from north to south.

Money matters

- Chief crops: coffee, sugar cane, soybeans, cocoa, beef, wheat, rice, maize.
- **Exports**: manufactured goods, iron ore, soybeans, footwear, coffee, beef.

Technology

- In 2005 there were about 60 million mobile phones in Brazil.
- There are more mobiles than landlines.
- Internet domain: .br

WORD BANK exports goods sold to other countries

Glossary

Amerindian person whose ancestors were the first people to live in South America

canopy covering provided by the tops of trees in forests

Catholicism a Christian religion. The Pope is head of the Roman Catholic Church.

Christian follower of the Christian religion. Christianity is based on the teachings of Jesus Christ

climate pattern of weather in an area

current steady flow of water

dam barrier across a waterway. It controls the flow of water.

drought long period of time without the usual amount of rainfall

environment the natural world or the conditions that surround us

exports goods sold to other countries

favela area of slums, or poor housing. Some of the houses are made out of scrap materials.

float platform, or stage, pulled by or built on to a vehicle. It is part of a carnival parade.

government group of people that makes laws and manages the country

humid when there is a lot of water vapour in the air

mine hole in the ground from which minerals such as metals, precious stones, or coal are dug

mineral natural substance found in rocks and in the ground. Metals and precious stones are minerals.

plain large area of flat country

plateau area of high, flat land

pollute to release harmful chemicals or waste into air, water, or soil

port place where ships load and unload goods or passengers

rainforest dense forest that has heavy rainfall

remote far from other places

republic form of government where there is usually a president

rural to do with the countryside

samba Brazilian dance with African origins

slave someone who is owned by another person

species different types of animals and plants

state area that can govern itself in some ways

tropical related to the tropics, the warmest parts of the world

volleyball game played by two teams. Players hit a ball over a high net with their hands.

wetlands area of watery land, such as marshes or swamps

Index